This book is dedicated to my dear friends Debbie and Jimmie Lustig
and also to my dear friend Marcy Blum.

Designing
with Flowers

PRESTON BAILEY

RIZZOLI
NEW YORK

New York · Paris · London · Milan

Photography by John Labbe

Table of Contents

Introduction

When I started in this business thirty-three years ago, I never imagined that what was then a newfound love of flowers would lead to career that is, in every way, my dream job. To spend my days creating one-of-a-kind events that serve as the backdrop of some of the most memorable moments of my clients' lives is an honor. Though my budgets and experience have grown, my tools have remained the same, and the most important tool I have is flowers. Their vibrant and elegant beauty is timeless and their versatility unparalleled. A table, tent, or ballroom can be transformed by the addition of flowers. A tablescape with an understated tablecloth and simple settings can morph into something far more opulent with the addition of an intricate floral arrangement. Flowers are a feast for the senses: vivid colors, unique textures, and signature scents all work together to transform a moment. But flowers do more than just delight the senses—they also tell a story. Whether playful, elegant, organic, or tailored, they serve as a form of self-expression for both designer and client. Those who know me know how much I enjoy having fun with floral design, whether it's a flower-covered ceiling that imparts the feeling of living in a garden or an unexpected floral sculpture that brings a sense of whimsy and joy to an otherwise serious occasion.

Whichever way they are showcased, floral designs bring an event to life. In *Designing with Flowers*, I will show you how I take a party from concept to execution. I will introduce you to some of my clients, the dreams they shared with me, and my interpretation of those dreams. It is my hope that you will enjoy looking through the images as much as I enjoyed creating the designs and that my creations will serve as a source of joy and inspiration as you design your own event. — Preston

Preston Bailey on his wedding day.

An Intimate Dinner for One Thousand Guests

When this very special client came to me, I was very impressed by her excellent taste. She was clear that she wanted a classic, traditional, and comfortable look to her wedding and that it would need to be a tented design. Fortunately, we live in a time when the technology behind tents is advanced enough to accommodate this kind of request. Yet there was still one major challenge: The bride-to-be wanted her one thousand guests to feel a real sense of intimacy. "How does one provide that in a gigantic tent?" I wondered, and I started to brainstorm.

After a bit of back-and-forth with my team, we decided to create two separate tents: one for a comfortable cocktail reception and another for an intimate sit-down dinner. As an expert in entertaining, my client wanted each area of the event to be properly decorated, including the entrance and all transitional areas, so we used a mixture of green and white flowers in each of those areas to tie them together.

In the vast cocktail tent, my team and I knew that we needed one major design element that would serve as an anchor. I had the idea of creating a life-size sculpture of a hot-air balloon made out of flowers. When placed against the cream- and white-colored furniture, this was the one statement piece that dealt with the height, width, and depth of the enormous tent.

For the tent that housed the dinner, we opted to create three different levels: a main level and one level to each side. We used a combination of round and rectangular tables and draped the entire tent in delicate fabric in order to achieve a softer atmosphere. Last, we placed my favorite decorative element: a structure that looked like three clouds of organic, cascading flowers. I believe these hanging sculptures contributed immensely to fostering the illusion of an intimate dinner party held in a very large space. The green carpet also served to ground the space.

Above and opposite: Decorating an entrance is the perfect way to create a feeling of celebration.

Opposite and below: A hot-air balloon sculpture composed entirely of flowers acted as a dramatic statement piece in the cocktail tent of this wedding.

Previous spread, above, right, and following spread: Diaphanous fabric and a few large floral sculptures hanging from the ceiling worked perfectly to create the illusion of intimacy at this dinner for one thousand guests. The centerpieces of varying heights also help.

Opposite, above, and following spread: Tall glass containers give the impression that the flowers are floating, while low arrangements provide interest at eye level.

European Elegance

GRAND HOTEL CAP DU FERRAT, THE SOUTH OF FRANCE

There are few things more romantic than getting married in the South of France amid the lavish grandeur of the *Grand Hotel Cap du Ferrat,* one of the world's most beautiful hotels. My bride, Mrs. Sarahmay Wesemael Robbins, chose this location for a very personal reason: she grew up in the area.

When Sarahmay arrived at my New York office, it was immediately clear that she was no ordinary bride. Not only was I was in awe of her impeccable taste in fashion, but her understanding of architecture and design was like no other. It was she, not I, who served as the driving force behind her elegant wedding. She had a desire for an understated elegance that would complement—not compete with—the beauty of the venue she and her fiancé had chosen. A lover of symmetry, she wanted the space to be balanced, and her attention to detail was unparalleled. For example, knowing that my offices are close to the flower district here in New York City, the bride, along with her lovely sister, Tamara, scoured the markets for a flower that had the color she wished to showcase at her wedding. Finally, after several hours, she found the perfect color: a very pale pink rose called "Quick Sand."

I have often said that the secret to my success is working with clients that inspire me. I can say without hesitation that Sarahmay was a great source of inspiration, not only for myself, but for those on my team as well. When we began constructing designs, they were a mix of traditional with a fresh "French twist." We presented the three different concepts to our bride and agreed on a final design that used the hotel's architecture as the base point for the "French-Inspired" design.

The ceremony was held inside of the hotel after which guests were escorted to a tennis court that we had transformed into a tended ballroom. The walls of the hotel were recreated inside of the tent with architectural boxwood. We added large archways and arched French doors to match the design of the property. We combined the boxwood walls with a glass ceiling and placed cherry blossoms around the room to bring the outdoors *inside.* Clear crystal chandeliers and mirrored sconces were placed around the space to add a level of sophistication. The dance floor was designed to look like an Aubusson rug and framed sentiments that were important to the bride and groom such as "eternal love," "passion," and "family."

Although designing this event was a pleasure, as with any event, there were also challenges. One of the things I have learned working around the world is the importance of planning for (and being sensitive to) the cultural differences in each country. While I love working in France, the custom of saying "no" until they have a very clear understanding of what is needed was a challenge in the beginning. It took me about a week to catch onto this, but once I did, it was smooth sailing. The result was a beautiful and joyful bride framed by a design she told me she loved. As a designer, you really cannot ask for more.

Above, opposite, and following spread: On the lawn of the Grand-Hôtel du Cap-Ferrat, on France's Côte d'Azur, we created a whimsical canopy of orchids above the aisle.

Above and opposite: For the gazebo, I enjoyed using flowers as an architectural detail.

Previous spread, above, and right: This magnificent ballroom stands in a tent on the hotel's tennis court. We used boxwood to create the lush green walls and added French windows to pay homage to the hotel's façade.

California Splendor

HOTEL GRAND DEL MAR, SAN DIEGO, CALIFORNIA

When I first sat down with Savannah Brinson, I was charmed by her grace and elegance. An accomplished interior designer, she had a very strong understanding of what she liked and didn't like, and she presented both to me in a remarkably gentle way. She and her fiancé, LeBron James, were very committed to making their guests feel comfortable at the event. The couple was clear that they wanted a dramatic ceremony, an inviting and intimate reception, and a black-and-white after-party.

My team and I began work on the designs immediately, but we faced the very difficult challenge of keeping everything a secret. Because of LeBron's celebrity status, it felt like thousands of journalists were aching to reveal the plans. The couple really wanted to have a private wedding and celebrate their union only with their family and closest friends, so we did everything we could to make that wish come true.

The design for the ceremony was clean and crisp with white, creams, and soft pink flowers. It included an altar enveloped by a giant floor-to-ceiling sculpture dripping with garlands of flowers. We used pillar candles as a backdrop for the altar, and floral trees marked the aisles while garlands cascaded off the chandeliers hanging from the ceiling.

The white walls, white floor, and white ceiling of the reception space were accented by colorful flowers and bright-hued tables in shades of purple, pink, blue, and green. We brought in a mix of traditional and modern elements that would be interesting to the couple and their guests: Louis XVI–style chairs and three-seater benches were embellished with purple rosettes and paired with more modern tables, such as a rectangular mirrored version and a round table upholstered in deep purple fabric that featured a mirrored center.

Images were projected onto the walls to give the space an architectural appearance. To further the classical illusion, we added oversized mirrors with thick gilded frames. I love the notion that we achieved the look of traditional architecture by using new technology. The projections changed as the night progressed and included whimsical images like fish and birds.

Designing this wedding was a delightful challenge, and we (myself, my team, and Lilit and Olga from Sky Events, with whom we collaborated) were thrilled to see the couple and their guests laughing and dancing throughout the night.

Previous spread, above, and right: In order to give the tent the illusion of a ballroom, we hung an elaborate floral chandelier over the dance floor.

Previous spread: We projected an image of a baroque hallway onto the blank walls of the tent to evoke the feeling of a grand historical space. Opposite and above: The fun part of using projections is that you can surprise the guests by changing the images from ornate to whimsical.

Previous spread, opposite, above, and following spread: I loved the difference between the light colors of the flowers and the dark wood of this hall.

White Place Settings

Many brides have grown up with the image of having a white wedding, and that often translates into a soft palette, which can be used to create an ethereal-looking event. White can look one-dimensional, but as a base, it's where the fun begins.

As a designer, I approach an all-white room as I would a blank canvas—I begin by adding simple layers, and I watch it come to life. There are endless opportunities to surprise guests by pairing white with softer pastels or accenting it with fantastic details, such as sparkling crystals or elegant metals that shimmer in the candlelight. In this section, I present the many different layers I have used to bring the beauty of white and pastels to life.

Above, below, and opposite: This over-the-top table design uses the subtle contrast between the cream and white hues to create dimension and depth.

Opposite: A tiered stand holds "cupcakes" made from flowers. Above: The conical vases taper toward the top and then explode in a frenzy of white petals.

Opposite, above, and below: A long floral arrangement snakes between candles and vases, and drapes elegantly off the table.

Above and opposite: A metal globe encrusted with candles is supported by a tree trunk wrapped with a creeping vine.

Above, below, and opposite: My client requested a winter wonderland setting to surprise and delight her guests at an intimate dinner.

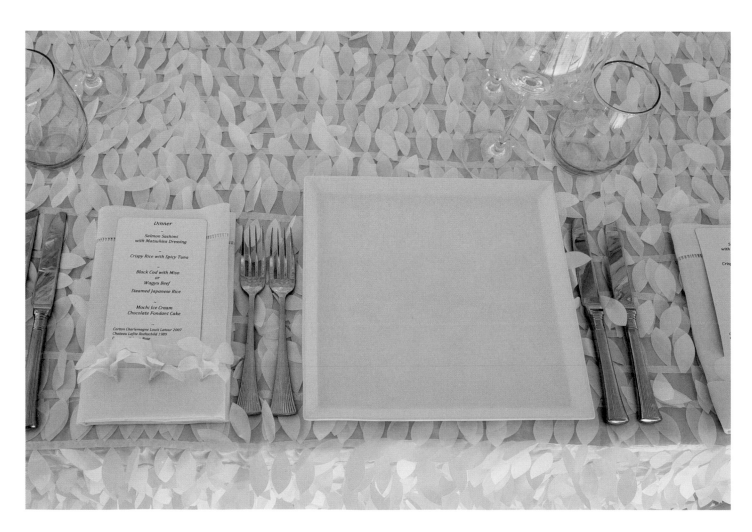

Dinner

*Salmon Sashimi
with Matsuhisa Dressing*

Crispy Rice with Spicy Tuna

*Black Cod with Miso
or
Wagyu Beef
Steamed Japanese Rice*

*Mochi Ice Cream
Chocolate Fondant Cake*

*Corton Charlemagne Louis Latour 2007
Chateau Lafite Rothschild 1989*

Opposite, above, and below: You can never go wrong with mini topiaries as your table arrangements.

Above: Small bouquets at each seat complement the table's centerpiece. Below and opposite: A whimsical lamp—with a floral lampshade—is larger than life.

Above and following spread: Shimmering tiers of crystals rain from these celestial centerpieces. Opposite: A pearl-encrusted candelabra is an elegant decoration.

A Royal Romance

THE MIDDLE EAST

A royal engagement led my crew and me on a fantastic eighteen-month journey after Her Royal Highness, the princess, reached out and asked me to design her wedding.

The princess shared my strong interest in design, so it's no wonder we clicked the moment we met. Our brainstorming sessions were inspiring, and although she had clear ideas as to the overall look and feel that she wanted, I was honored that she gave me a lot of latitude to play with the details. There was a bit of trial and error, but eventually we created exactly what she desired. She was very precise in her vision.

We chose a palette of white, cream, and soft pinks, ensuring that her wedding would be not only royal but also very romantic. The baroque foyer area included Rococo paintings of people in love embellished by floral frames and whimsical Murano chandeliers hanging from the ceiling. Custom-made gold and cream sofas and vintage chairs were placed around the foyer.

During the ceremony, the bride was revealed on a gold-framed stage and appeared from beneath a giant chandelier made from crystals and flower petals. She then walked down a serpentine Plexiglas aisle that was more than 320 feet long and covered a pool of water to give guests the illusion that she was walking on water. A complementary serpentine lighting installation above the aisle featured individual fiber-optic teardrop-shaped lights and was designed by artist Bruce Munro. Onstage, the bride sat on a kosha wedding couch under a 20-foot-tall cherry blossom tree with thousands of branches that held crystal-encased votives and crystals. A hillscape backdrop behind the princess was covered with more crystals and one thousand orchid blooms.

The lavish reception was a feast for the eyes and senses. I have always had a love for French parterre gardens, so I suggested creating such a garden on the ceiling of the reception area. Her Royal Highness was surprised but then delighted by the whimsical idea. Two giant crystal cakes were placed under the design to represent sculptures that might be found in a magical garden. To bring the garden to life, we adorned each dining table with different collections of floral birdcages. Guests danced, dined, and enjoyed themselves until nine o'clock the next morning. It was a big day, indeed!

Previous spread: A cherry blossom tree cascades delicately over the altar. Opposite and above: Her royal highness's aisle was made of flowers and water.

Above and opposite: For her dramatic entrance on stage, her royal highness was concealed under the gigantic floral and crystal chandelier.

Above and opposite: The entrance lobby of the wedding was adorned with Rococo-style artwork framed by fresh flowers. A collection of Murano glass chandeliers added a touch of playfulness. Following spread: I have always loved the beauty of a manicured parterre. For the dining room, I suggested to her royal highness that she should create such a garden on the ceiling. The Parterre Garden acted as an art installation.

Opposite and above: The dinner centerpieces were floral birds—a peacock for the buffet and caged birds for the tables. Following spread: A royal place setting.

Heaven
on Earth

THE RITZ CARLTON, DORADO BEACH, PUERTO RICO

One of the best parts of my job is being able to sit with each client and channel what's in his or her mind. Two things keep me going after all these years: the joy of knowing that no two events are the same and the challenge of bringing my clients' vision to vivid, unforgettable life.

When bride-to-be Amber came into my office with her mother, Loren, I was immediately taken by her kind spirit. Young and in love with her fiancé, Duane, Amber shared her vision for a one-of-a-kind destination wedding. "I want my ceremony to look like a garden in heaven," she said. I began to imagine what heaven might look like in her mind. Most people envision heaven as the ultimate paradise, so this meant that the couple's 250 guests should feel as if they were surrounded by unparalleled beauty. I was starting to plan in my head when Amber looked at me and asked, "Can you make it happen in five weeks?" Without missing a beat, I smiled and said, "Of course, I can."

I called a meeting with my staff, and we spent the following weeks working diligently to bring the couple's vision to life. Like me, the bride adored flowers, and she also adhered to a "more is better" approach. We used pastel colors, like peaches and pinks, throughout the design, pairing them with antique gold and silver used as neutrals.

The ceremony, held in the spa of the newly renovated Ritz-Carlton Dorado Beach, in Puerto Rico, featured a platform over a reflecting pool. Being a spiritual person, Duane wanted the ceremony to have a more religious feel, so we placed a floral cross at the altar. For the cocktail reception, Amber wanted a glamorous atmosphere with one of my crystal trees.

The reception tent was built on the fairway of the resort's golf course—the whole fairway! After cocktails, guests were ushered into the dining area of the tent, which held my favorite design element: a gigantic floral and crystal chandelier placed above the painted dance floor, anchoring the space.

As I stood there, watching everyone enjoy the celebration thrown by this lovely couple, I could not help but be proud of my amazing staff. More than 150 people worked tirelessly, transporting thousands of flowers and facing a number of challenges, and we were rewarded with happy guests and a happy couple. Amber and Duane were also utterly delighted by the surprise performances of Mary J. Blige, Maxwell, and Marc Anthony, who all sang live at their reception.

Previous spread: The bride wanted her ceremony to look like "a garden in heaven." Opposite: The bride's and groom's first initials were made from flowers floating in a pool of water. Above: Because the spiritual aspect of the ceremony was important to the groom, we created a floral cross for the altar.

Opposite and above: In the cocktail tent, the bride had requested one of my crystal trees, and we placed it in the center of the bar to serve as a focal point.

Above: A sweeping fleur-de-lis made from roses held guests' seating arrangement cards. Opposite: Floral wall topiaries made a dramatic statement in the entrance foyer. Following spread: A projected image of spring illuminated the reception tent, which was flanked by candlelight designs on either side.

Above and opposite: The bride adheres to my "more is better" approach when it comes to flowers, and I incorporated peach and pink hues to pair with items in antique gold and silver that I used as neutrals. Following spread: A gigantic floral and crystal chandelier anchored the dance floor in the reception tent.

A Joyful Celebration

NEW DELHI, INDIA

When I met the father of the groom, I found his enthusiasm and joy absolutely infectious. He had a mind-set of the more, the merrier when it came to planning the wedding of his son and his son's beautiful bride, something I found to be not only generous but also beautiful and inspiring.

Now, it is no secret that I love surprising my guests throughout the night, and this family shared my passion for giving guests the unexpected over the course the evening. In fact, they wanted their guests to feel as though they were moving through a large park that had something new to enjoy at every turn. It soon became clear to me that this would be an event in every sense of the word—and a joyful one at that. My team and I soon began working on transforming a big open field into a city of dreams for the couple and their guests, who numbered nearly four thousand.

We created an architectural gateway made from thousands of bamboo sticks and showcased a life-size floral elephant sculpture. A large center stage with the backdrop of a stylized elephant was used for a number of incredible performances that took place during the theater-style reception.

And the dining arrangement was the most amazing part: We created a small village with settings that made it look like there were four different restaurants. Guests were asked to sit where they pleased and simply enjoy the evening. A small "petting zoo" composed of a number of floral animals was displayed at the dessert station, and guests ordered cocktails from a large ice bar. Alongside the bar were ice sculptures of iconic buildings that represented all the locations from which guests had traveled to attend the event—another special detail provided by the host.

I have to say, this was one of the most fun designs I have ever done. I thoroughly enjoyed working with the family and having the chance to learn a great deal about Indian culture. Indian weddings are celebratory events that last for a few days and often include vibrant and lively ceremonies. I truly came back from this event a changed man.

Previous spread: A spectacular revolving seating area for the bride and groom. Opposite: An oversize floral lounge mirrored the crimson color of the guests' chairs. Below, left, right, and bottom: The wedding was in an open space, which made it a perfect place for a floral petting zoo, which served as a festive backdrop for photos.

Above: Sculpting with petals can be lots of fun, and I covered some of my favorite glass shapes with cymbidium orchid petals. Opposite: Elongated centerpieces burst with warm colors and cascading amaranthus flowers.

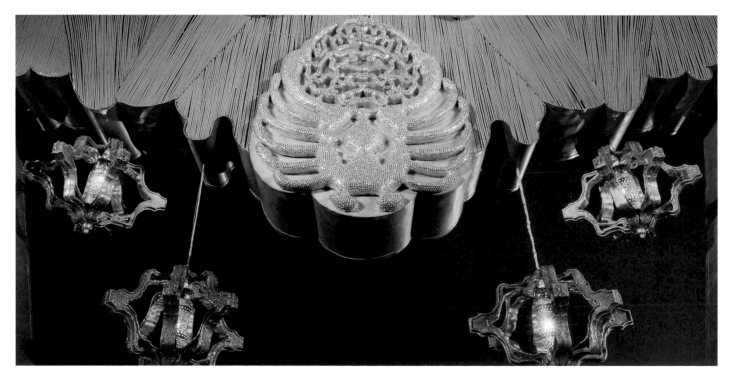

Clockwise from top left: The theme of the event was an elephant walk, and to greet the guests, we built a gigantic entrance made from bamboo. Guests were met by a life-size floral elephant striding gracefully in a bed of flowers. Details of the crystal entrance design.

This spread: The celebration featured a very unique dining experience. We created a plaza with four different restaurants, each one delineated by its design. Guests could pick the restaurant of their choice, sit, and order what they liked.

Above: Indian weddings are known for their amazing shows. Following the elephant theme, we created a stage that employed new, innovative technology. Opposite: In order to ensure the bride and groom remained the focal point of the celebration, we created a crystal tree that revolved very slowly as the night progressed. Following spread: Sculptures of iconic buildings representing the locations from which guests had traveled to attend the event.

Colorful Place Settings

When picking the colors for your next event, allow personal taste to be your guide. Choosing color is mostly about adding a splash of self-expression, and there is no such thing as a right or a wrong color palette.

Growing up in Panama, with its lush concentration of tropical, vibrant hues, predisposed me to seek out the magic of color. The key is to combine colors in an interesting and synergistic way that is pleasing to the eye; my approach is often to work with hues that are part of the same family. However, at times, creating contrast can also be exciting. In this section, I share a number of color combinations and designs, some simple and others a little more complex, in the hope that you will find inspiration when choosing a palette for your own wedding or party.

Opposite: The orchids in the place setting echo the centerpiece. Above: This peacock centerpiece has a lavish floral tail.

Opposite, above, and below, left and right: An item as simple as a lantern makes a great statement on your table. You can either give it an antiqued look, with vines spiraling upward, or you can opt for a classic metal version.

Above, below, and opposite: Hanging orchids are entwined with delicate fiber-optic lights in this glistening centerpiece.

Above and below: This display features a sea of orchids in a variety of beautiful colors.

Above and below: LED lighting is the perfect way to enhance your centerpiece.

Opposite and above: A metal support covered by tree bark and wrapped with vines gives the illusion of a living tree.

Previous spread and opposite: The greens and purples achieve beautiful contrast. Above: An ornate wooden frame acts as the base for this cascading floral display.

Opposite and above: Hanging crystal garlands give the effect of a weeping willow tree.

Opposite and above: Covering a glass vase with sequined fabric makes this arrangement shimmer.

Above, below, and opposite: The bride and groom's table is bedecked with flowers and features a brilliant tree overhead.

Above and opposite: The metal base of this centerpiece is covered with sequined fabric to make it shine.

Opposite and above: When there is no opportunity to hang something from the ceiling, one can create a chandelier that is supported by the table.

Opposite: Some of the details in this arrangement are made using sugar flowers to give another layer of depth to the piece.
Above and below: This gorgeous table has a design that encloses the flowers within a ring of flickering candles.

Above and opposite: The crystal vase and the crystal tabletop seemingly merge into one.

Opposite, above, and below: Soft pastel colors foster a calm atmosphere.

Opposite, above, and below: Pedestals decorated with flowers and crystals adorn the centerpiece on this table.

Opposite and above: Tiers of delicate crystals give this traditional arrangement a modern twist.

Opposite, above, and below: This classic table features a single large centerpiece flanked by two candelbra and multiple smaller centerpieces.

A Summer Garden Wedding

SOUTHAMPTON, NEW YORK

One of the things I enjoy most about working in private residences is that I get a chance to incorporate elements that are meaningful and personal to the clients and their home. For this particular wedding, I had worked with the bride's mother and father previously, and I was honored when I was asked to design their daughter's special day.

The bride and her parents met me in my New York studio, and we began discussing her vision. She wanted her wedding to marry classic comfort with modern warmth and be accented by traditional elements, such as crystal chandeliers, glass, and boxwood. We agreed that there should be a synergy between the garden ceremony and the reception. The bride's mother, who has amazing attention to detail, told me she liked the idea of using the color blue, and I agreed. "As you know, I have a very specific shade in mind. It would be fun to have the glass tabletops made in that color," she said. Earlier that week, she had picked one of the hydrangeas from her garden and sent it to me to ensure I knew just which shade to use. I not only appreciated her attention to detail, I loved the color.

Knowing that my client and her family wanted to be involved in every step of the process, I had them send me images of things they loved and then incorporated those ideas into my renderings. Before we knew it, we had a full design!

The ceremony was being held outdoors, and we created a setting that would complement their beautiful gardens where the aforementioned hydrangeas were blooming. We decided to blend those flowers into the design by lining the aisle with a low side runner made from boxwood topped with hydrangeas. The walls of the reception tent were designed to showcase French windows. As the bride wanted to have a more glamorous feel for this part of the event, we added a mirrored proscenium at the bandstand in order to frame the stage.

We loved the design, but the execution posed a bit of a challenge. It rained the entire week before the wedding! Of course, we were all nervous that we'd have to put the rain plan in motion, but we were greeted by clear skies the day of, and the beautiful bride and glowing groom were able to exchange vows in perfect weather.

Previous spread, above, and opposite: My clients wanted a ceremony that worked with their summer garden, so we incorporated hydrangeas into the design of the aisles and the altar. Following spreads: The reception tent was enclosed in boxwood walls, and to highlight the stage, we added a mirrored proscenium.

Tasteful Whimsy

HOTEL KEMPINSKI, JAKARTA, INDONESIA

When I met this wonderful bride, I was impressed not only by her impeccable fashion sense but also by her generosity. She was very clear that she wanted her guests to experience a romantic and fun night, and she wanted to spoil them and her husband—whom she had arranged a special cake for—with various surprises throughout the reception.

A fan of romance and whimsy, the couple wanted to juxtapose elegant elements with those that were more modern, and ensure that no matter what, everyone fully enjoyed themselves.

The white and pewter color theme was carried throughout the event, from the romantic dinner to the fun after-party celebration. For the reception, we created a mosaic-like stage design with shelves that were filled with floral arrangements. To the delight of guests, each was allowed to take one arrangement home as a gift. Blame it on my passion for detail, but I could not help but incorporate a few floor-to-ceiling floral basket-weave columns to complement the fluted centerpieces.

As I am quite partial to art installations, I wanted to create my version of one for the after-party and have it be an eye-catching statement piece that honored both the bride and groom. Using thousands of lightbulbs, we made the words "double happiness" in Chinese on the ceiling. The sculpture, then, was not solely a subtle message to the couple—it also served as the main design anchor in the fun-filled after-party room.

Previous spread: The stage was flanked by shelves filled with floral arrangements; each guest was allowed to take one home. Opposite, above, and following spread: My client wanted simplicity, and I gave her that. However, I could not resist creating a few oversize floral columns to emphasize the ballroom's tall ceilings.

Below and opposite: I am always fascinated by art installations, and for this wedding's after-party, I wanted to introduce a cultural element. Utilizing thousands of lightbulbs, we spelled out the phrase "double happiness" in Chinese characters on the ceiling.

A Fantasy
in the Forest

As soon as the lovely bride, Alexandra, entered my office, I knew this would be a unique wedding. Not only did she share my passion for incorporating the beauty of Mother Nature, but she was also looking to create a magical world. When I met her fiancé, Sean, I was amazed by his ability to visualize an event down to each detail. He knew what his wedding should look like and feel like. I have to admit, it was very exciting to be working with clients who took such an interest in seeing their exact vision come to life. I looked forward to collaborating with designer Ken Fulk on this challenge.

Because the couple wanted the event to take place in a secret location among the trees, it was essential that the flowers look natural and organic. My team started working on possible locations immediately, and finding the perfect space proved very difficult. After a few weeks, we found what I consider one of the most naturally beautiful locations in the world: a redwood forest. We then began working with Ken's team on larger-than-life designs that would stand out against such a remarkable backdrop. Mother Nature was there, shining in all of her splendor.

The day of the wedding, guests—in full costume—were escorted under an archway of flowers to an enormous iron gate. After everyone had a glass of champagne, the gate opened, and the group passed through a floral curtain, down a secluded path, and over a man-made bridge that we had covered in plants and flowers. Guests then entered a petting zoo that featured horses, rabbits, and chickens. An hour later, they were led down a path that had been densely covered with 300,000 white rose petals. Finally, the guests arrived at a ruined castle, where the ceremony took place.

The couple exchanged vows under a very old tree that was several hundred feet tall. We designed the space to make it look as though hundreds of flowers were growing up the tree and hanging from it in 20- to 30-foot-long wispy white ribbons. After the ceremony, guests were led through a maze and then under an arch to the entrance of the dining section. There stood a 30-foot-long dragon sculpted out of leafy plants and flowers.

In the reception area, the bride and groom sat at a table made from wood and crystals, with custom bronze-and-iron legs, and the centerpieces were each a little different and featured tall, branchy bases crowned with flowers and garlands. As a designer who loves natural and organic elements, working on this event was a dream come true.

Previous spread: Guests in costume crossed this bridge bedecked with garlands of flowers on their way to the ceremony. Above, opposite, and following spread: The bride and groom exchanged vows in front of an ancient redwood tree that was several hundred feet tall.

Opposite and above: Designer Ken Fulk, with whom I collaborated, created giant pots overflowing with garlands to complement the beauty of the environment.

Opposite and above: Guests were led under flower-encrusted arches and along a pathway covered with white rose petals to get from the cocktail area to the ceremony. Following spread: The dining area continued the theme of magic and fantasy that surrounded the wedding.

Above and right: A night view of the ceremony area. Following spread: This bridge was created specifically for the event to serve as an entrance for the guests.

Above, left and right: Transitional spaces featured items like a sculpture of a large cross and a topiary tree. Opposite: The feeling of magic permeated the forest as guests walked through the event along a pathway covered in a carpet of rose petals.

Opposite and above: An arch in the back of a whimsical floral dragon served as an entrance to the dining area. Following spread: Lights changed the mood at night.

Acknowledgments

Eckhart Tolle once said, "If the only prayer you ever say in your entire life is *thank you*, it will be enough." I find great inspiration and solace in this quote as I believe gratitude is the greatest giver of gifts and the greatest gift we can give one another.

There are so many friends, colleagues, and clients without whom this book would not have been possible, and while thanking everyone would take a book in itself, I want to express my gratitude to all of those I have worked with, worked for, and who have worked for me. In addition, I would like to make special mention of the following people who helped me with this project.

First, I want to thank my partner and husband, Theo Bleckmann. You are my truest fountain of inspiration and I love and appreciate you in ways that extend far beyond words.

My friend and agent, Jill Cohen. Thank you for keeping me focused and helping me to bring this book to life.

Deepest thanks to my Rizzoli family and my publisher, Charles Miers for allowing me to put my vision on paper. I am ever grateful.

Thank you, Kathleen Jayes, for your guidance and patience with all of the last-minute changes.

I want to express my appreciation and gratitude to my book designer, Sam Shahid and his assistant Danny Lori, for their amazing ability to display my work in the best possible way.

Very few people understand how difficult it is to shoot an event, sometimes in just five minutes. To my friend and photographer, John Labbe, I say thank you for always giving 100% and getting that perfect shot.

My love and appreciation goes out to all of my supportive clients. Without you, there would be no "PB Designs."

My gratitude also goes to my editor and friend, Brenda Della Casa. Brenda, very few can organize the words in my head on paper as well as you do. Thank you for helping this Panamanian verbally express his ideas better than he can.

My gratitude goes to my executive assistant, Patrick Suwat Laorawat. Thank you for always being there for me and helping to keep my life in order.

To all of my colleagues at PB Designs: Anne Crenshaw, Xoua Vang, Kelly Irwin Rutty,Caleb Wertenbaker, Nikita Polyanski, Jee Young Sim, Christina Gonzalez, Piero Manrique, Luiz Fernando Leite, Eduardo Martins, Carlos Belo Jr., Pedro Santos, Kathy Romero, Tamara Speid Bowden, Samantha Hayden, Sanaw Ledrod, Kesanee Ortiz, Oscar Simeon Jr., I say a big thank you. You are my family. We fight, we play, we even work endless hours, always with one thing in mind: To do our very best. My deepest gratitude goes to every single one of you.

Thank you to my beloved family: My sisters, Aminta Duncan and Olivia St Louis. My beloved nieces and nephews, Belinda Duncan, Bernadette Peters, Bernard Duncan, Zellerita McKnight, Michael St Louis, Dina Duncan, and Marissa St Louis. Also my thanks go to all of my grand-nieces and nephews: Daivon Peters, Delano Peters, Jasmine McKnight, Christine McKnight, Isaiah McKnight, Aliyah St Louis, Quianna Duncan. My cousins, Beverly Chase and Pearl Goode.

To my dear friends, your support means the world to me. Joan Rivers, Nadine Jervis, The Keidans, Sylvia Weinstock, Ayiri Oladunmoye in Nigeria, Reem Acra, Bershan Shaw, Ritva Haukemaa, Gloria Dare, Regina Evans, my late friend Mr Bill Ash, Peter Azrak, Vicente Wolf, Erwin Gonzales, Stacey Madison, Arndt Oesterle, Ira Levy, Franklin Gonzalez and Raul Melo, Liz Newmark, Mr. & Mrs. Lisjanto Tjiptobiantoro (Mr. & Mrs. Meity), Dani Soegiarso, Richard & Jane Novick, Tamara Wesemael, Darcy Miller Nussbaum, Fiona Jackson, Lilit Khachaturian, Tifany Wunschl, Valerie Romanoff, Darren Olarsch, Felipe Ossio, Jackie James, Carlos Andres, Harriette Rose Katz, Catherine Whitworth, Sheila Johnson, Arndt Oesterle, Arturo De Noriega, Dave Cox, Se Yang, Joy Agness, Lana Volodymyr, Barbara Diez de Tejada, Pauline Hoogmoed, Leticia Guerra, Roger Thomas, Susan Magrino thank you.

In closing, I want to thank you, my readers, for believing in my work, and God, for allowing me the opportunity to do what I love every day of my life.

A special thank you to the following:
Photographers:
Robert Evans, South of France bride image
Ira Lippke, South Hampton bride and groom image
Christian Oth, Big Sur, CA bride and groom image
Roger Grasas, three little girls at the royal wedding in the Middle East image
Maike Schulz, winter wonderland floral ceiling and wall treatment images

Asia: Ferns N Petals, Ade Sari, Adi Tent, A-Ling, Alvin Soo, Anita Suhartono, Bina Flora, Dani Soegiarso, Davirex Enterprises, Dina Touwani, Donny Hardono, DSS Sound System, Eka Deniarti, Ekram Ali, Emil Eriyanto, Etcetera Entertainment, Felicia Cokrowibowo, Floralines, Ghia Sekar, Hamid, Hestoi Nurartri, Hotel Indonesia Kempiski,

Inet Leimena, Toto Arto, Iwan Hutapea, Jimmy Pandie, Made Arsana, Magenta Orchestra, Michael Gunardi, Poppy Hanady, Production Plus, PT Bina Flora Lestari, PT Grand Indonesia, PT Multi Kreasi Enterprise, Rina Indriani Halin, Sendy Wildiani, Sima Augusta, Stupa Caspea, Toto Arto, Tri Reka Dinamis, Ully Roesly Hajersa, Yenie Trika, Royal Base Corporation, Davirex Enterprises

Europe: Bruce Munro, Deco-Flame Live Productions, Fiorella SARL, Roni-Fleurs, Galliano Ferro

Middle East: Raymond Chouity Weddings, Rose Classic, Fiona Jackson, The Event Hub, Creative Technology, Delta Sound, Dubai Artistic, Evolution Events, IBS Stage Sets, Top Carpet, Ghazwan Makiha, Shadi Maatoq, Vissionnaire.

United State: 28th Street Marketplace, A & R Sewing Co, Accent Décor, Afloral, Alan Party & Tent Rentals, Arthur Backal, Artistic Ribbon, Atomic Arts, Avalon Tent and Party, B & J Florist Supply, Bazar Fabrics, Beta Iron Works, Better Mousetrap, Bhens Products Co, Biederman & Sons, Body Vox, Boutross Co, Bravura Glass & Mirror, Cake Alchemy, Caramoor Center for Music and the Arts, Central Floral Supply, Classic Party Rentals, Creative Engineering, Daytona Trimming, Decorating Studio, Di Fiore Eventos, Duenas Trailers, Dutch Flower Line, E-Klectix, Eliel's Catering Services, Ellen Weldon, EM-BEE ideas, Erin Halley, Exihibit Floral Studio, Flora by Arquetipo, Frank A. Suarez, Fusion, G & G Distributors, G. Page Wholesale Flowers, G2 Audio and Lighting, Gabrielle Jaworskyj, Gio Draping Events, Glow Concepts, Go Productions Services, Great Foods Marketing Company, Great Performances, Green Light Booking, Hillcrest Garden, Hire Elegance, Hi-Tech Events, Holiday Flower & Plants, Igmor Crystal Lite, Iqbal Hayder, J. Van Vliet, Jamali Garden Supplies, KierChris Productions, Kits and Expendables, Lancy Jewelry, Lasting Art, Lea Brumage, Levy Lighting, Liba Fabrics, Lighting Design, Lilit Khachaturian, Lins International Co, Luxe Event, Marcy Blum, Mayesh Wholesale lorist, Michael Curry, Michelle Rago, Momental Designs, Nadine Jervis, National Tool Griding, New York Golf Center, Nuage Designs, NYC Displays, Okamoto Studio, Olga Garabekyan, Olivier Chang Catering and Events, Pablo Oliveira, Paper Works & Events, Paradise Candles, Party Brights, Party Crashes, Party Line, Party Rentals, Perfect Endings, Piedmont Travel, Planter Resource, PSL Productions, Rick Blink, R & F Fabrics, Sam Godfrey, Shaker Group, SK Floral, Sky Events and Production, Something Different Party Rental, Starr Tent, State of the Art enterprises, Sunpride, Sylvia Weinstock Cakes, The Container Store, Trans-Ocean Enterprises, Tri-State Crating, United Wholesale Florist, US Evergreens, Vase Source, Vivia Costalas, Weddingstar.com, West Elm, Wichie Sound Performance, Wizard Studios North, YRC Freight, Shutterfly, Robert Evants Studio, On the move, Untitled Film Works, Clos Bu Val, Starlight Orchestras, Martha Stewart Weddings, Chandon, Great Performances, Sweet by Jana, Baume & Mercier, Chocolate Moderne, Kusmi Tea, Michael Lambert, Anielly Machado, Amelia Belo, Alex Ruiz, Angkhana Chermisirivatana, Atithan Easumang, Cesar Ugarte, Dennis Delsignore, Felipe Silva, Frank Ornowski, Hui Ju Chang, Kujtim Rexha, Pongpanvadee Jinda, Samorn Panpinyo, Marjeth Cummings, Michael Nolan, Sherwin Mahon, Siravit Ratanakomol Terrance Singleton Sr, Rene Aguilar, Yessid Ortiz

Top row, left to right: Michael Ruiz, Production Assistant; Tamara Speid Bowden, Office Manager; Xoua Vang, CEO; Luiz Fernando Leite, Director of Operations; Piero Manrique, Designer; Anne Crenshaw, CFO; Caleb Wertenbaker, Design Director; Michael St. Louis, Production Assistant; Robert D'Alessandro, Florist

Second row, left to right: Nikita Polyansky, Production Designer; Farrah Zhao, WEB Editorial Intern; Brenda Della Casa, WEB Editor-in-Chief; Samantha Hayden, Wedding & Event Planning Assistant; Kathy Romero, Director of Wedding and Event Planning; Kelly Irwin Rutty, Director of Production; Marjeth Cummings, Florist; Sanaw Ledrod, Director of Floral Design; Mona (June's baby girl)

Third row (bottom, left to right): Rachel Leva, WEB Marketing & Advertising Intern; Kate Pangilinan, WEB PR & Social Media Intern; Pedro Santos, Production Tech Support; Carlos Belo Jr., Traffic Manager; Eduardo Martins, Production Manager

Top row, left to right: Sherwin Mahon, Florist; Michael Kravitz, Florist; Michael Nolan, Florist; Alex Ruiz, Florist; Oscar Simeon Jr., Senior Floral Designer; Terrance Singleton Sr., Florist; Cesar Ugarte, Florist; Abraham Gonzalez, Production Tech Support

Second row, left to right: Samorn Panpinyo (Gai), Florist; Atithan Easumang (June), Florist; Hui Ju Chang (Lulu), Florist; Yessid Ortiz, Florist; Kesanee Ortiz (Kay), Director of Floral Production; Pongpanvadee Jinda (Apple), Florist; Angkhana Chermisirivatana (Katie), Florist

Third row (bottom, left to right): Christina Gonzalez, Design Director; Felipe Silva, Production Tech Support; Siravit Ratanakomol (Malik), Production Tech Support; Oranicha Stein (Moo), Florist; Suwat Laorawat (Patrick), Executive Assistant to Preston Bailey

First published in the United States of America in 2014
by Rizzoli International Publications, Inc.
300 Park Avenue South New York, NY 10010
www.rizzoliusa.com

Photography by John Labbe

2014 2015 2016 2017 / 10 9 8 7 6 5 4 3 2 1

Distributed in the U.S. trade by Random House, New York

Printed in China

ISBN-13: 978-0-8478-4246-9
Library of Congress Catalog Control Number: 2013948616

Design by Sam Shahid